ZBIGNIEW HERBERT

1924–1998

WHERE did Herbert come from; where did his poetry come from? The simplest answer is: We don't know. Just as we never know where any great artist comes from, irrespective of whether they are born in the provinces or in the capital.

Zbigniew Herbert, born in Lwów [then Poland] in 1924, led a life that especially in his youth was full of adventure and danger, though one is tempted to say that he was created rather for a quiet existence between museum and library. There are still many things we do not know about the wartime period of his life — to what extent he was engaged in the resistance, or what he experienced during the occupation. We know that he came from what is called in English the "middle classes," and in Polish is known as the intelligentsia. The relative, or perhaps truly profound, orderliness of his childhood was destroyed once and for all in September 1939 by the outbreak of war.

When the war ended and Lwów was incorporated into the territory of the Soviet Union, Herbert was one of thousands of young people living in abeyance, trying to study, and hiding their underground past. The whole time up till 1956, when a political thaw altered the situation for the better, Herbert led an unsettled existence, changing addresses frequently, moving around between Gdańsk, Warsaw, Toruń, and Kraków, and taking on various jobs (when he was short of money he even sold his own blood, a painfully accurate metaphor for the life of a poet). He studied philosophy, wondering whether or not he should devote himself to it full time. He was also drawn to art history. For political reasons he was unable to bring out his first book of poetry, but he began to publish individual poems and book reviews. The year 1956, as I mentioned, changes almost everything for Herbert. His debut, *Chord of Light*, is enthusiastically received. Suddenly, thanks to the thaw, the borders of Europe are open to him, to some extent at least; he can visit France, Italy, London. From this moment there begins a new chapter in his life, one that was to last almost to his final months — he died in July 1998.

drawings in this book come from Zbigniew Herbert's sketchpads

Every great poet lives between two worlds. One of these is the real, tangible world of history, private for some and public for others. The other world is a dense layer of dreams, imagination, fantasms. Herbert's dreams are sustained by various things — travels, Greece and Florence, the work of great painters, ideal cities (which he saw only in the past, not in the future, unlike many of his contemporaries). But they are also sustained by the knightly virtues of honor and courage. In him we find two central intellectual problems — participation and distance. He never forgot the horror of war and the invisible moral obligations he incurred during the occupation. He himself spoke of loyalty as a leading ethical and aesthetic yardstick. And in the poems and essays the tragic poet steps out alongside the carefree Mr Pickwick, who does not imagine that he has deserved such a great misfortune. It may be here that there lies the particular, indefinable charm of both Herbert's poetry and his essays — this tragicomic mixing of tones, the fact that the utmost gravity in no way excludes joking and irony. But the irony mostly concerns the character of the poet, or that of his porte-parole Mr Cogito, who is by and large a most imperfect fellow.

While as concerns the message of this poetry — and it is poetry with a message, however obscure — the irony does not affect it whatsoever. The paradox of Herbert, which is perhaps especially striking in our modern age, also resides in the fact that though he refers willingly and extensively to existing "cultural texts" and takes symbols from the Greeks and anywhere else, it is never in order to become a prisoner of those references and meanings — he is always lured by reality.

This poetry is about the pain of the twentieth century, about accepting the cruelty of an inhuman age, about an extraordinary sense of reality. And the fact that at the same time the poet loses none of his lyricism or his sense of humor — this is the unfathomable secret of a great artist.

ADAM ZAGAJEWSKI

NR **4524**
1700/8
946

NOS RECTOR

ET

DECANUS COLLEGII PROFESSORUM

FACULTATIS *iuris et oeconomiae*

UNIVERSITATIS COPERNICIANAE THORUNIENSIS

hac tabula profitemur testatumque esse volumus,

Domin*um* *Herbert Zbigniew*

oriund*um* *Leona*

in album

UNIVERSITATIS COPERNICIANAE THORUNIENSIS

FACULTATIS *iuris et oeconomiae*

rite relat*um* esse. Eius rei fidem nomina ipsa subscripsimus

Thorunii, die **3** mensis *Ianuarii* 19 *48*

Rector
Universitatis Copernicianae
Thoruniensis

Decanus Collegii Professorum
Facultatis

Własnoręczny podpis właściciela książeczki

gniew Herbert's student record book, Nicolaus Copernicus University in Toruń, 1948

róż *na papier*

Vézelay   Muzeum bezcarski

wieczór pełny mgieł i smutku

cmentarz zielone kwiaty

Kościół św Magdaleny

    pomoc: jak doznania mistyczne

    łóż, żali; trwać : biel

    kamień: światło

    źródło żywności

    Tuk spełnień

    milczenie

    tylko wielkie

    i spienione
    milczenie boże

Rzeczywistość może
uczłowiać Vézelay

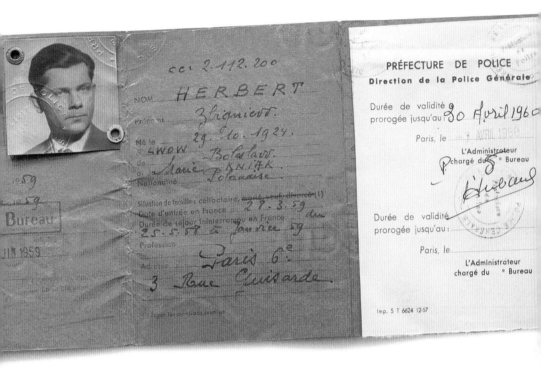

Imp. S T 6624 12-57

WHAT kind of poet is Zbigniew Herbert? Is he difficult? Is he hard to follow, hard to scan, impossible to remember? Look at "Pebble" and decide for yourself.

What kind of poem is this, and what is it all about? About nature, perhaps? Perhaps. I, for one, though, think that if it is about nature, then it is about human nature. About its autonomy, about its resistance, about, if you will, its survival. In this sense it is a very Polish poem, considering that nation's recent, more exactly, modern, history. And it is a very modern poem, because Polish history, one may say, is modern history in miniature — well, more exactly, in a pebble. Because whether you are a Pole or not, what history wants is to destroy you. The only way to survive, to endure its almost geological pressure, is to acquire the features of a pebble, including the false warmth once you find yourself in somebody's hands.

Herbert is a poet of tremendous ethical consequence because his verse zeroes in on the cause, not just the effects, which he treats as something incidental. Which they always are. Symptoms are not the malaise.

In this sense, he is a historical poet. His pen often summons history, which is after all the mother of culture, in order to enable his reader to endure and, with luck, to overcome the vulgarity of the present. His poems show that most of our beliefs, convictions, and social concepts are in bad taste, if only because they are entertained at someone else's expense. He is a supreme ironist, of course; to me, though, his irony is but the safety valve of his compassion, since human tragedy is repetitive.

JOSEPH BRODSKY   1987 Nobel Prize Winner

I FEEL a deep affinity with his writings. He was over thirty when his first book of poems appeared. Before 1956 the price for being published was to renounce one's own taste and he did not want to pay it. If the key to contemporary Polish poetry is the collective experience of the last decades, Herbert is perhaps the most skillful in expressing it and can be called a poet of historical irony. He achieves a sort of precarious equilibrium by endowing the patterns of civilization with meanings, in spite of all its horrors. History for him is not just a senseless repetition of crimes and illusions, and if he looks for analogies between the past and the present, it is to acquire a distance from his own times. His theory of art is based upon the rejection of "purity": to the imperturbable Apollo he opposes the howling, suffering Marsyas, though his own reticent poetry is the opposite of a howl.

CZESŁAW MIŁOSZ   1980 Nobel Prize Winner

Potęga smaku

Pani Profesor
Izydorze Dąmbskiej

To wcale nie wymagało wielkiego charakteru
nasza mężność mizerota i upór
mieliśmy odrobinę niezbędnej odwagi
lecz w gruncie rzeczy było to sprawa smaku

Tak smaku
w którym są włókna duszy i chrząstki sumienia

kto nie polubił nas lepiej i piękniej kuszono
słano kobiety różowe płaskie jak opłatek
lub fantastyczne stwory z obrazów Hieronima Boscha
lecz piekło w tym czasie było byłe jakie
dół mokry zaułek morderców barak
zwany pałacem sprawiedliwości

zmajstrowany Mefisto w leninowskiej kurtce
wysyłał w teren wnuczęta Aurory
chłopców o twarzach ziemniaczanych
bardzo brzydkie dziewczyny o czerwonych rękach

Ich retoryka parobków była nie do zniesienia
(Marek Tuliusz obraca się w grobie)
zamiłowanie do tautologii bara pojęć jak cepy
żadnej dystynkcji w rozumowaniu
puste ekektomorze składnia pozbawiona urody koniunktiwu

Tak więc estetyka może być pomocna w życiu
nie należy zaniedbywać nauki o pięknie
~~Trzeba mieć Grecy jedno jest źródło dobra: tego co nadobne~~   pół bóg...

Zanim zgłosimy akces trzeba pilnie badać
Kształt architektury z danie kolory urzędowe
niekształtne skale bezradki rytm rat pogrzebów   milczymy

Księżyska naszych zmysłów wybrały dumne wygnanie
To wcale nie wymagało wielkiego charakteru
mieliśmy tylko odrobinę niezbędnej odwagi
lecz w gruncie rzeczy było to sprawa smaku

Tak smaku
który każe wyjść skrzywić się wycedzić szyderstwo
choćby za to miał spaść bezcenny kapitel ciała
głowa.

Zbigniew Herbert with the heroine of Solidarity, Anna Walentynowicz, 1981. The 25th anniversary of tł workers' protests in Poznań, which were bloodily suppressed by the communist regime

*B*ARBARIAN *in the Garden* is an ironical title. This "Barbarian" who makes his pilgrimage to the sacred places is steeped in the culture and history of classical and medieval Europe, and even though there is situated at the centre of his consciousness a large burnt-out zone inscribed "what we have learned in modern times and must never forget even though we need hardly dwell upon it," this very consciousness can still muster a sustaining half-trust in man as a civilizer and keeper of civilizations. The book is full of lines which sing out in the highest registers of intellectual rapture.

But Herbert never gets too carried away. The ground-hugging sturdiness which he recognizes and cherishes in archaic buildings has its analogue in his own down-to-earth-ness. His love of "the quiet chanting of the air and the immense planes" does not extend so far as to constitute a betrayal of the human subject, in thrall to gravity and history.

Herbert always wants to probe past official versions of collective experience into the final ring of the individual's perception and endurance. He does so in order to discover whether that inner citadel of human being is a selfish bolt hole or an attentive listening post. To put it another way, he would not be all that interested in discovering the black box after the crash, since he would far prefer to be able to monitor the courage and conscience of each passenger during the minutes before it.

Zbigniew Herbert is a poet with all the strengths of an Antaeus, yet he finally emerges more like the figure of an Atlas. Refreshed time and again by being thrown back upon his native earth, standing his ground determinedly in the local plight, he nevertheless shoulders the whole sky and scope of human dignity and responsibility.

SEAMUS HEANEY   1995 Nobel Prize Winner

DIE UNIVERSITÄT WIEN VERLEIHT AUF BESCHLUSS
DES KURATORIUMS DEN

GOTTFRIED-VON-HERDER-PREIS

DER VON DER STIFTUNG F.V.S. ZU HAMBURG
FÜR VERDIENSTVOLLES WIRKEN IM SINNE EINER
FRIEDLICHEN VERSTÄNDIGUNG UNTER DEN VÖLKERN
ZUR VERFÜGUNG GESTELLT WURDE, FÜR DAS JAHR 1973

HERRN

ZBIGNIEW HERBERT

WARSZAWA

ER HAT ALS LYRISCHER UND DRAMATISCHER DICHTER
TRAUM UND ERFAHRUNG, MYTHOS UND RATIO,
WÖRTER UND SACHEN, ZEITEN UND SYSTEME IN EIN
ÄSTHETISCHES GLEICHGEWICHT GEBRACHT UND DARIN
DURCH DIE STILLE KRAFT BESTÄNDIGER GEDANKEN-
ARBEIT WIRKSAM ERHALTEN.

SEINE PHILOSOPHIE IST DICHTERISCH WIE EIN POEM,
SEINE DICHTUNG IST KLAR WIE EIN PHILOSOPHISCHER
DIALOG, EIN BEITRAG ZU EINER SPRACHE, IN DER SICH
DIE WELT VERSTÄNDIGEN WIRD.

ALS EINER, DER SICH, WIE GOETHE ES WOLLTE, VON
DREITAUSEND JAHREN RECHENSCHAFT ZU GEBEN
WEISS, HAT ER DIE FRÜCHTE DES ABENDLÄNDISCHEN
GEISTESLEBENS WAHRLICH NICHT ALS „BARBAR"
GEPLÜNDERT, SONDERN ALS GÄRTNER GEPFLEGT
UND GEMEHRT.

DIESE URKUNDE IST AUSGESTELLT
AM TAGE DER FEIERLICHEN ÜBERGABE DES PREISES.

WIEN, AM 3. MAI 1973

REKTOR DER UNIVERSITÄT   VORSITZENDER DES KURATORIUMS

BUNDESMINISTERIUM FÜR UNTERRICHT

AUF EINHELLIGEN ANTRAG
DER JURY VERLEIHE ICH
ZBIGNIEW HERBERT
FÜR DAS LYRISCHE SCHAFFEN
DEN ÖSTERREICHISCHEN
STAATSPREIS FÜR
EUROPÄISCHE LITERATUR
ALS INTERNATIONALEN
NIKOLAUS LENAU · PREIS
WIEN · AM 25 · OKTOBER 1965

DER BUNDESMINISTER FÜR UNTERRICHT:

TO MARCUS AURELIUS

To Professor Henryk Elzenberg

Good night Marcus put out the light
and shut the book For overhead
is raised a gold alarm of stars
heaven is talking some foreign tongue
this the barbarian cry of fear
your Latin cannot understand
Terror continuous dark terror
against the fragile human land

begins to beat It's winning Hear
its roar The unrelenting stream
of elements will drown your prose
until the world's four walls go down
As for us? — to tremble in the air
blow in the ashes stir the ether
gnaw our fingers seek vain words
drag off the fallen shades behind us

Well Marcus better hang up your peace
give me your hand across the dark
Let it tremble when the blind world beats
on senses five like a failing lyre
Traitors — universe and astronomy
reckoning of stars wisdom of grass
and your greatness too immense
and Marcus my defenseless tears

lomas for prizes awarded to Zbigniew Herbert: Internationaler Nikolaus Lenau Preis (Vienna 1965),
ann Gottfried von Herder Preis (Vienna 1973)

ANSWER

It will be a night of deep snow
thick enough to muffle steps
deep shadow changing bodies
into two puddles of darkness
we're lying holding our breath
even thought's lowest whisper

if wolves don't track us down
or a man in a fur coat cradling
fast-shooting death on his chest
we'll have to jump up and run
amid a din of short dry salvos
to that longed-for other shore

everywhere earth is the same
it teaches wisdom everywhere
a man is weeping white tears
mothers are cradling children
the moon is beginning to rise
and building us a white house

It will be a night after hard waking
the conspiracy of the imagination
tastes of bread is light as wodka
yet every dream of palm trees
confirms our choice to stay here

the dream is cut off by three tall
rubber-and-iron men who enter
check your name check for fear
and order you down the stairway
not allowing you to take a thing
but a guard's compassionate face

Hellenic Roman medieval
Indian Elizabethan Italian
probably French above all
a bit of Weimar Versailles
we lug so many homelands
on one back on one earth

but the one homeland I'm sure
to keep in the singular is here
where you're trod into the mud
or with a proudly ringing spade
they dig a fair hole for longing

A KNOCKER

There are those who grow
gardens in their heads
paths lead from their hair
to sunny and white cities

it's easy for them to write
they close their eyes
immediately schools of images
stream down from their foreheads

my imagination
is a piece of board
my sole instrument
is a wooden stick

I strike the board
it answers me
yes — yes
no — no

for others the green bell of a tree
the blue bell of water
I have a knocker
from unprotected gardens

I thump on the board
and it prompts me
with the moralist's dry poem
yes — yes
no — no

THE ENVOY OF MR COGITO

Go where the others went before to the dark boundary
for the golden fleece of nothingness your last reward

go upright among those who are down on their knees
those with their backs turned those toppled in the dust

you have survived not so that you might live
you have little time you must give testimony

be courageous when reason fails you be courageous
in the final reckoning it is the only thing that counts

and your helpless Anger — may it be like the sea
whenever you hear the voice of the insulted and beaten

may you never be abandoned by your sister Scorn
for informers executioners cowards — they will win
go to your funeral with relief throw a lump of earth
a woodworm will write you a smooth-shaven life

and do not forgive in truth it is not in your power
to forgive in the name of those betrayed at dawn

beware however of overweening pride
examine your fool's face in the mirror
repeat: I was called — was there no one better than I

beware of dryness of heart love the morning spring
the bird with an unknown name the winter oak
the light on a wall the splendor of the sky
they do not need your warm breath
they are there to say: no one will console you

Keep watch — when a light on a hill gives a sign — rise and go
as long as the blood is still turning the dark star in your breast

repeat humanity's old incantations fairy tales and legends
for that is how you will attain the good you will not attain
repeat great words repeat them stubbornly
like those who crossed a desert and perished in the sand

for this they will reward you with what they have at hand
with the whip of laughter with murder on a garbage heap

go for only thus will you be admitted to the company of cold skulls
to the company of your forefathers: Gilgamesh Hector Roland
the defenders of the kingdom without bounds and the city of ashes

Be faithful Go

~~Posłanie Pana Cogito~~
Przesłanie

Idź dokąd poszli tamci ? do ciemnego kresu
po złote runo nicości po swoją ostatnią nagrodę
Idź wyprostowany ~~wśród~~ pośród tych co na kolanach
wśród odwróconych plecami i obalonych w proch

ocalałeś nie poto aby żyć
masz mało czasu trzeba dać świadectwo

bądź odważny gdy rozum zawodzi bądź odważny
w ostatecznym rachunku jedynie to się liczy
a Gniew twój bezsilny niech będzie jak morze
ilekroć usłyszysz głos ! poniżonych i bitych

niech nie opuszcza ciebie twoja siostra Pogarda
dla szpiclów katów tchórzy — oni wygrają
pójdą na twój pogrzeb i z ulgą rzucą grudę
a kornik napisze twój uładzony życiorys

I nie przebaczaj ! zaiste nie w twojej mocy
przebaczać w imieniu tych ! których zdradzono o świcie

Strzeż się jednak ~~dumy~~ oschłości niepotrzebnej
oglądaj w lustrze swą błazeńską twarz
powtarzaj : zostałem powołany — czyż nie było lepszych

Strzeż się ~~oschłości~~ oschłości serca kochaj źródło zaranne
ptaka o nieznanym imieniu dąb zimowy
światło na murze splendor nieba
one nie potrzebują twego ciepłego oddechu
są poto aby mówić : nikt cię nie pocieszy

APOLLO AND MARSYAS

The real duel of Apollo
with Marsyas
(absolute ear
versus immense range)
takes place in the evening
when as we already know
the judges
have awarded victory to the god

bound tight to a tree
meticulously stripped of his skin
Marsyas
howls
before the howl reaches his tall ears
he reposes in the shadow of that howl

shaken by a shudder of disgust
Apollo is cleaning his instrument

only seemingly
is the voice of Marsyas
monotonous
and composed of a single vowel
A

in reality
Marsyas relates
the inexhaustible wealth
of his body

bald mountains of liver
white ravines of aliment
rustling forests of lung
sweet hillocks of muscle
joints bile blood and shudders
the wintry wind of bone
over the salt of memory

shaken by a shudder of disgust
Apollo is cleaning his instrument

now to the chorus
is joined the backbone of Marsyas
in principle the same A
only deeper with the addition of rust

this is already beyond the endurance
of the god with nerves of artificial fibre

      along a gravel path
      hedged with box
      the victor departs
      wondering
      whether out of Marsyas' howling
      there will not some day arise
      a new kind
      of art — let us say — concrete

suddenly
at his feet
falls a petrified nightingale

he looks back
and sees
that the hair of the tree to which Marsyas was fastened
is white

completely

ELEGY OF FORTINBRAS

To C.M.

Now that we're alone we can talk prince man to man
though you lie on the stairs and see no more than a dead ant
nothing but black sun with broken rays
I could never think of your hands without smiling
and now that they lie on the stone like fallen nests
they are as defenseless as before The end is exactly this
The hands lie apart The sword lies apart The head apart
and the knight's feet in soft slippers

You will have a soldier's funeral without having been a soldier
the only ritual I am acquainted with a little
There will be no candles no singing only cannon-fuses and bursts
crepe dragged on the pavement helmets boots artillery horses drums drums
                                                    I know nothing exquisite
those will be my manoeuvres before I start to rule
one has to take the city by the neck and shake it a bit

Anyhow you had to perish Hamlet you were not for life
you believed in crystal notions not in human clay
always twitching as if asleep you hunted chimeras
wolfishly you crunched the air only to vomit
you knew no human thing you did not know even how to breathe

Now you have peace Hamlet you accomplished what you had to
and you have peace The rest is not silence but belongs to me
you chose the easier part an elegant thrust
but what is heroic death compared with eternal watching
with a cold apple in one's hand on a narrow chair
with a view of the ant-hill and the clock's dial

Adieu prince I have tasks a sewer project
and a decree on prostitutes and beggars
I must also elaborate a better system of prisons
since as you justly said Denmark is a prison
I go to my affairs This night is born
a star named Hamlet We shall never meet
what I shall leave will not be worth a tragedy

It is not for us to greet each other or bid farewell we live on archipelagos
and that water these words what can they do what can they do prince

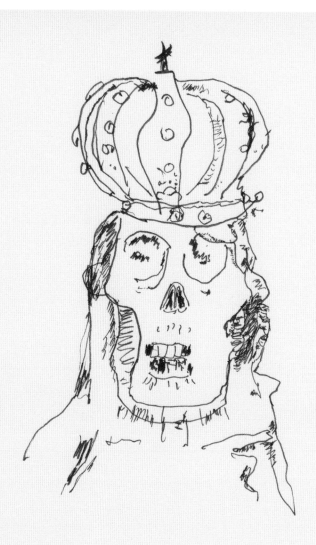

kari b

WHY THE CLASSICS

To A.H.

1

in the fourth book of the Peloponnesian War
Thucydides tells among other things
the story of his unsuccessful expedition

among long speeches of chiefs
battles sieges plague
dense net of intrigues of diplomatic endeavors
the episode is like a pin
in a forest

the Greek colony Amphipolis
fell into the hands of Brasidos
because Thucydides was late with relief

for this he paid his native city
with lifelong exile

exiles of all times
know what price that is

2

generals of the most recent wars
if a similar affair happens to them
whine on their knees before posterity
praise their heroism and innocence

they accuse their subordinates
envious colleagues
unfavorable winds

Thucydides says only
that he had seven ships
it was winter
and he sailed quickly

if art for its subject
will have a broken jar
a small broken soul
with a great self-pity

what will remain after us
will be like lovers' weeping
in a small dirty hotel
when wallpaper dawns

PEBBLE

The pebble
is a perfect creature

equal to itself
mindful of its limits

filled exactly
with a pebbly meaning

with a scent which does not remind one of anything
does not frighten anything away does not arouse desire

its ardor and coldness
are just and full of dignity

I feel a heavy remorse
when I hold it in my hand
and its noble body
is permeated by false warmth

    — Pebbles cannot be tamed
    to the end they will look at us
    with a calm and very clear eye

NIKE WHO HESITATES

Nike is most beautiful at the moment
when she hesitates
her right hand beautiful as a command
rests against the air
but her wings tremble

For she sees
a solitary youth
he goes down the long tracks
of a war chariot
on a gray road in a gray landscape
of rocks and scattered juniper bushes

that youth will perish soon
right now the scale containing his fate
abruptly falls
toward the earth

Nike would terribly like
to go up
and kiss him on the forehead

but she is afraid
that he who has never known
the sweetness of caresses
having tasted it
might run off like the others
during the battle

Thus Nike hesitates
and at last decides
to remain in the position
which sculptors taught her
being mightily ashamed of that flash of emotion

she understands
that tomorrow at dawn
this boy must be found
with an open breast
closed eyes
and the acid obol of his country
under his numb tongue

MR COGITO AND THE IMAGINATION

1

Mr Cogito has never trusted
the tricks of the imagination

the piano at the top of the Alps
played concerts false to his ear

he had no regard for labyrinths
the Sphinx filled him with disgust

he lived in a cellarless house
without mirrors or dialectics

jungles of tangled images
were never his homeland

he rarely got carried away
on the wings of a metaphor
he then plunged like Icarus
into the arms of the Great Mother

he adored tautologies
explanations
idem per idem

a bird is a bird
slavery slavery
a knife a knife
death is death

he loved
a flat horizon
a straight line
earth's gravity

2

Mr Cogito
will be counted
among the species *minores*

he will receive indifferently
the verdict of men of letters

he employed the imagination
for wholly different purposes

he wanted to make of it
an instrument of compassion

he longed to understand fully

— Pascal's night
— the nature of a diamond
— the prophets' melancholy
— the wrath of Achilles
— the fury of mass murderers
— the dreams of Mary Stuart
— the fear of Neanderthals
— the last Aztecs' despair
— Nietzsche's long dying
— the Lascaux painter's joy
— the rise and fall of an oak
— the rise and fall of Rome

in order to revive the dead
and maintain the covenant

Mr Cogito's imagination
moves like a pendulum

it runs with great precision
from suffering to suffering

there is no place in it
for poetry's artificial fires

he wants to be true
to uncertain clarity

THE POWER OF TASTE

For Professor Izydora Dąmbska

It did not take any great character
our refusal dissent and persistence
we had a scrap of necessary courage
but essentially it was a matter of taste
                    Yes taste
which has fibers of soul and the gristle of conscience

Who knows if we'd been better more prettily tempted
sent women pink and flat as wafers
or fantastic creatures out of Hieronymus Bosch
but what did hell look like in those days
a mud pit a cutthroat's alley a barracks
called a Palace of Justice
a moonshine Mephisto in a Lenin jacket
sent Aurora's grandchildren into the field
boys with potato-eaters' faces
very ugly girls with red hands

Truly their rhetoric was just too shoddy
(Marcus Tullius turned in his grave)
chains of tautologies a few flailing concepts
torturers' dialectics reasoning without grace
syntax devoid of the beauty of the subjunctive

So in fact aesthetics can be an aid in life
one shouldn't neglect the study of beauty

Before we assent we must examine closely
architectural forms rhythms of drum and fife
official colors the homely rituals of burial

        Our eyes and ears refused to submit
        our princely senses chose proud exile

It did not take any great character
we had a scrap of necessary courage
but in essence it was a matter of taste
                    Yes taste
which tells you to walk out wince spit out your scorn
even if for that your body's precious capital the head
                    would roll

Potęga smaku

Pani Profesor
Izydorze Dąmbskiej

To wcale nie wymagało wielkiego charakteru
nasza nieugiętość niezgoda i upór
mieliśmy odrobinę koniecznej odwagi
lecz w gruncie rzeczy była to sprawa smaku
                    Tak smaku
w którym są włókna duszy i chrząstki sumienia

Kto wie gdyby nas lepiej i piękniej kuszono
słano kobiety różowe płaskie jak opłatek
lub fantastyczne twory z obrazów Hieronima Boscha
lecz piekło w tym czasie było ~~było~~ jakie
dół mokry zaułek morderców barak
nazwany pałacem sprawiedliwości
samogonny Mefisto w leninowskiej kurtce
posyłał w teren wnuczęta Aurory
chłopców o twarzach ziemniaczanych
bardzo brzydkie dziewczyny o czerwonych rękach

Zaiste
~~ich~~ retoryka ~~parobków~~ była ~~nie do zniesienia~~   aż nazbyt parciana
/ Marek Tuliusz obracał się w grobie /
~~zamiłowanie do~~ tautologii parę pojęć jak cepy
dialektyka ~~byłów~~ żadnej dystynkcji w rozumowaniu
~~puste eksklamacje~~ składnia pozbawiona urody koniunktiwu

Tak więc estetyka może być pomocna w życiu
nie należy zaniedbywać nauki o pięknie
Zanim zgłosimy akces trzeba pilnie badać
kształt architektury rytm bębnów i piszczałek
kolory oficjalne nikczemny rytuał pogrzebów

Nasze oczy i uszy odmówiły posłuchu
książęta naszych zmysłów wybrały dumne wygnanie

REPORT FROM A BESIEGED CITY

Too old to carry arms and fight like the others —

I was mercifully given the supporting role of a chronicler
I write down — not knowing for whom — a siege's history

I have to be precise but I don't know when the siege began
two centuries ago in December September dawn yesterday
we here are all suffering from the loss of a sense of time

we were left only the place and an attachment to the place
we govern ruins of temples ghosts of gardens and houses
if we lose our ruins we will be left with nothing

I write as best I can in the rhythm of these endless weeks
Monday: stores are empty a rat is now the unit of currency
Tuesday: the mayor has been killed by unknown assassins
Wednesday: cease-fire talks the enemy interned our envoys
we don't know where they are that is where they were shot
Thursday: after a stormy meeting a majority of votes rejected
the motion of the local merchants for unconditional surrender
Friday: plague broke out Saturday: N.N. a staunch defender
committed suicide Sunday: no water we resisted an assault
at the eastern gate the one called the Gate of the Covenant

I know it's all monotonous it won't move anyone to tears

I avoid comment emotion keep a tight rein write on facts
it appears only facts have value on the foreign markets
but with a kind of pride I long to bring news to the world
of the new breed of children we raised owing to the war
our children don't like fairy tales they have their fun killing
waking and sleeping they dream of soup of bread and bone
just like dogs and cats

in the evening I like to wander along the edges of the City
skirting the borders of our uncertain liberty
I watch from above an ant procession of troops their lights
I listen to the noise of drums and the barbarians shrieking
it is truly beyond me why the City is still defending itself

the siege is taking a long time our enemies have to take turns
nothing unites them apart from the desire for our destruction
Goths Tartars Swedes Caesar's men ranks of the Transfiguration
who can count them
the banners change their colors like a forest against the horizon
a delicate bird yellow in spring through green to winter's black

then in the evening freed from the facts I can meditate
on ancient questions remote ones for instance about our
allies across the sea I know they feel sincere compassion
they send flour sacks encouragement lard and good advice
they don't even know it was their fathers who betrayed us
they were our allies from the time of the second Apocalypse
the sons are blameless deserve gratitude so we are grateful

they have not lived through a siege long as an eternity
they who are touched by misfortune are always alone
defenders of the Dalai Lama the Kurds and the Afghans

now as I write these words those who favor appeasement
have acquired an advantage over the party of the staunch
an ordinary mood swing the stakes are still being weighed

cemeteries are growing the number of defenders shrinking
but the defense continues and it will continue to the end

and if the City falls and one man survives
he will carry the City inside him on the paths of exile
he will be the City

we look into hunger's face the face of fire face of death
the worst of all — the face of betrayal

and only our dreams have not been humiliated

1982

ONE OF THE DEADLY SINS OF CONTEMPORARY CULTURE IS THAT IT pettily avoids a frontal confrontation with the highest values. Also the arrogant conviction that we can do without models (both aesthetic and moral), because our place in the world is supposedly so exceptional and can't be compared with anything. That's why we reject the aid of tradition and stumble around in our solitude, digging around in the dark corners of the abandoned little soul.

There exists a false view to the effect that tradition is like a fortune, a legacy, which you inherit mechanically, without effort, and that's why those who object to inheritance and unearned privileges are against tradition. But in fact every contact with the past requires an effort, a labor, and a difficult and thankless labor to boot, for our little "I" whines and balks at it.

I have always wished that I would never lose the belief that great works of the spirit are more objective than we are. And they will judge us. Someone very rightly said that not only do we read Homer, look at frescoes of Giotto, listen to Mozart, but Homer, Giotto and Mozart steal looks at us, eavesdrop on us and ascertain our vanity and stupidity. Poor utopians, debutants of history, museum arsonists, liquidators of the past, are like those madmen who destroy works of art because they cannot forgive them their serenity, dignity and cool radiance.

"The Little Soul" [extract], in: *The Labyrinth on the Sea*

THE INVESTIGATION, HOWEVER, WAS OVER AND THE ENVOYS OF CLEMENT V assisted passively at the passing of the sentence. The leaders of the Templars faced life imprisonment. The sentence of Jacques de Molay and Geoffroi de Charney was read in Notre-Dame Cathedral. A great crowd listened in silence; but before the reading of the sentence could be completed, both men — perhaps the dignified Gothic of Notre-Dame exercised its influence — faced the people and shouted down the charges of crime and heresy levelled against the Templars whose rule "was always sacred, right and Catholic." A sentry's heavy hand fell on the mouth of the Master to muffle the last words of the condemned. The cardinals handed over the recalcitrant to the court of Paris. Philip the Fair commanded burning at the stake on the same day. To appease his anger, he gave to the flames another thirty-six unrepentant brothers.

High Jury, that appears to be the end of the drama of the Templar Order. Experts rummage the tombs for a clue to the mystery. Sometimes they come across the gifts of eternity, sometimes they are fascinated by the smile of the alleged Baphomet found on a portal. The defence set forth a more modest task: examination of the tools.

In history nothing remains closed. The methods used against the Templars enriched the repertoire of power. That is why we cannot leave this distant affair under the pale fingers of archivists.

"Defence of the Templars" [extract], in: *Barbarian in the Garden*

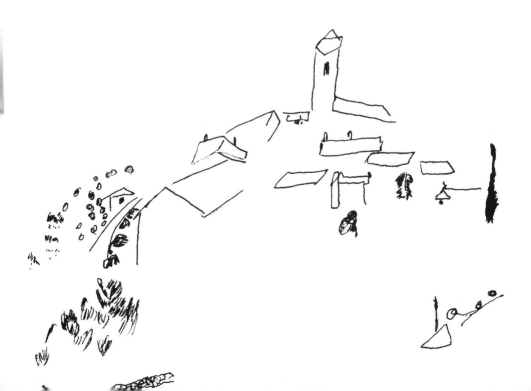

TULIPOMANIA — THE MOST EXTRAORDINARY BOTANICAL FOLLY WE know — was an episode inscribed on the margin of Great History. We have chosen it not without reason. It should be honestly confessed: we have a strange liking for presenting follies in the sanctuaries of reason, and we also like to study catastrophes against a gentle landscape. There are reasons more important than frivolous personal or aesthetic inclinations, however. For doesn't the affair we have described remind us of other, more dangerous follies of humanity that consist in the irrational attachment to a single idea, a single symbol, or a single formula for happiness?

This is why we cannot put a large period after the date 1637 and consider the matter definitively closed. It is not reasonable to erase it from memory, or count it among the inconceivable fads of the past. If tulipomania was a kind of psychological epidemic, and this is what we believe, the probability exists — bordering on certainty — that one day it will afflict us again in this or another form.

In some Far Eastern port it is getting ready for the journey.

"The Bitter Smell of Tulips" [extract], in: *Still Life with a Bridle*

Roger V. d. Weyden

Norman Fruman and Zbigniew
Herbert, California State College,
Los Angeles, 1970

Zbigniew Herbert's Dienstausweis
and Ausweis, Lwów 1943.
Documents issued by the German
occupation authorities

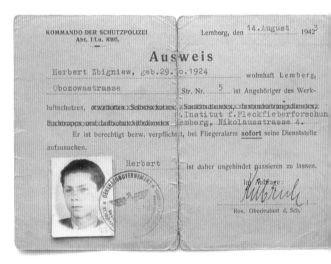

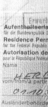

SERIA PH NR 264380

Zbigniew Herbert (born October 29, 1924 in Lwów, died July 28, 1998 in Warsaw) — Polish poet, essayist, dramatist and author of radio plays. Economist and lawyer by training, he also studied philosophy. During the Second World War he was a member of the resistance movement. He published his first volume of poems, *Chord of Light*, only in 1956, following the events of the Polish October when the Stalinist repressions had been softened. From 1958, he often stayed abroad, living mainly in Paris and Berlin, from where he ventured frequently to Italy, Greece, the Netherlands, Austria and England. In the 1970–71 academic year, he taught modern literature as visiting professor at the California State College in Los Angeles.

Author of 9 volumes of poems (the best known are: *Study of the Object, Mr Cogito, Report from a Besieged City*).

His volumes of essays *The Labyrinth on the Sea, Barbarian in the Garden* and *Still Life with a Bridle* make an extraordinary story of "the golden age" of European art and civilization.

Prize-winner of many international awards, including: Internationaler Nikolaus Lenau Preis (Vienna 1965), Johann Gottfried von Herder Preis (Vienna 1973), Petrarca-Preis (Verona 1979); Jerusalem Prize for the Freedom of the Individual in Society (Jerusalem 1991), Preis der SWR-Bestenliste (Baden-Baden 1994), T.S. Eliot Award for Creative Writing, awarded by The Ingersoll Foundation (USA 1995); Preis der Stadt Münster für Europäische Poesie (Münster 1997).

Zbigniew Herbert's works have so far been translated into 35 languages.

igniew Herbert's passport, 1986–92

On July 10, 2007 the Sejm (Parliament) of the Republic of Poland declared the year 2008 as the Year of Zbigniew Herbert. The resolution reads:

On the 10th anniversary of the death of the poet Zbigniew Herbert, one of the most outstanding writers of our times, the Sejm (Parliament) of the Republic of Poland has decided to pay tribute to the artist, who — creatively referring to the great tradition of European culture — enriched and strengthened it.

In times of a crisis of values and painful despondency, he stood firmly on the side of values: in arts — the canon of beauty, hierarchy and craft, in life — ethical codes, clearly separating the notions of good and evil. For many, he was a tragic and steadfast writer, an embodiment of faithfulness — to himself and the word.

Courageous and free-thinking, he expressed in his poetry the love for freedom, the faith in the dignity of the individual and its moral strength. He perceived patriotism as tough love, non-idealizing and requiring from those who profess it, not only sacrifice but also enlightened criticism, not only noble gestures but also hard work and responsibility.

He introduced into the Polish language an expression — commandment, the words "Be faithful Go."

Being deeply assured of the exceptional value of his literature, the Sejm (Parliament) of the Republic of Poland hereby declares the year 2008 as the Year of Zbigniew Herbert.

POETRY

Struna światła (*Chord of Light*). Warsaw, Czytelnik 1956.
Hermes, pies i gwiazda (*Hermes, Dog and Star*). Warsaw, Czytelnik 1957.
Studium przedmiotu (*Study of the Object*). Warsaw, Czytelnik 1961.
Napis (*Inscription*). Warsaw, Czytelnik 1969.
Pan Cogito (*Mr Cogito*). Warsaw, Czytelnik 1974.
Raport z oblężonego miasta i inne wiersze (*Report from a Besieged City and Other Poems*). Paris, Instytut Literacki 1983.
Elegia na odejście (*Elegy for the Departure*). Paris, Instytut Literacki 1990.
Rovigo. Wrocław, Wydawnictwo Dolnośląskie 1992.
Epilog burzy (*Epilogue to a Storm*). Wrocław, Wydawnictwo Dolnośląskie 1998.

PLAYS

Dramaty (*Plays*). Warsaw, PIW 1970. Including: *Jaskinia filozofów* (*The Cave of Philosophers*), *Rekonstrukcja poety* (*Reconstruction of a Poet*), *Drugi pokój* (*The Second Room*), *Lalek*.

ESSAYS

Barbarzyńca w ogrodzie (*Barbarian in the Garden*). Warsaw, Czytelnik 1962.
Martwa natura z wędzidłem (*Still Life with a Bridle*). Wrocław, Wydawnictwo Dolnośląskie 1993.
Labirynt nad morzem (*The Labyrinth on the Sea*). Warsaw, Fundacja Zeszytów Literackich 2000.
Król mrówek (*The King of the Ants*). Kraków, Wydawnictwo a5 2001.

PRESS ARTICLES

Węzeł gordyjski oraz inne pisma rozproszone (*The Gordian Knot and Other Scattered Writings*). Warsaw, Biblioteka Więzi 2001.

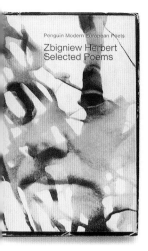

Selected Poems. Translated by Czesław Miłosz and Peter Dale Scott. Harmondsworth, Middlesex, Penguin Books 1968; reprinted by Carcanet (Manchester) in 1985 and by The Ecco Press (New York) in 1986.

lected Poems. Translated with an introduction and notes by John and Bogdana arpenter. Oxford, Oxford University Press 1977.

Barbarian in the Garden. Translated by Michael March and Jarosław Anders. Manchester, Carcanet 1985; reprinted by Harcourt Brace Jovanovich (San Diego) in 1986.

port from the Besieged City and Other Poems. anslated with an introduction and notes by John d Bogdana Carpenter. New York, The Ecco Press 1985; printed by Oxford University Press (Oxford) in 1987.

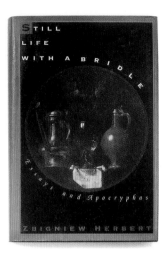

Still Life with a Bridle. Essays and Apocryphas. Translated by John and Bogdana Carpenter. New York, The Ecco Press 1991; reprinted by Jonathan Cape (London) in 1993 and by Vintage (New York) in 1994.

Mr Cogito. Translated by John and Bogdana Carpenter. New York, The Ecco Press 1993; reprinted by Oxford University Press (Oxford) in 1993.

Elegy for the Departure and Other Poems. Translated by John and Bogdana Carpenter. Hopewell, The Ecco Press 1999.

The King of the Ants. Mythological Essays. Translated by John and Bogdana Carpenter. Hopewell, The Ecco Press 1999.

The Collected Poems. 1956–1998. Translated and edited by Alissa Valles, with additional translations by Czesław Miłosz and Peter Dale Scott, introduction by Adam Zagajewski. New York, Ecco 2007.

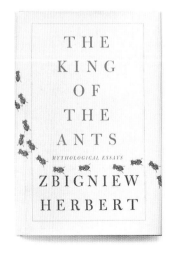